MANIFESTOS FOR THE 21ST CENTURY

SERIES EDITORS: URSULA OWEN AND JUDITH VIDAL-HALL

Free expression is as high on the agenda as it
has ever been, though not always for the
happiest of reasons. Here, four distinguished
writers address the issue of censorship in a
complex and fragile world where people with
widely different cultural habits and beliefs are
living in close proximity, where offence is easily
taken, and where words, images and behaviour
are coming under the closest scrutiny.
These books will surprise, clarify and provoke
in equal measure.

Index on Censorship is the only international
magazine promoting and protecting free
expression. A haven for the censored and
silenced, it has built an impressive track record
since it was founded 35 years ago, publishing
some of the finest writers, sharpest analysts and
foremost thinkers in the world. In this series
with Seagull Books, the focus will be on
questions of rights, liberties, tolerance,
silencing, censorship and dissent.

Without

luding religious orthodoxies, it ceases to exist. La

ion cannot be imprisoned, or art will die, and with it, a little of what r

s human. What is freedom of expression? Without the freedom to offer

eases to exist. Without the freedom to challenge, even to satirise all ort

es, including religious orthodoxies, it ceases to exist. Language

and the imagination cannot be imprison

or art will die, and with it, a little o

what makes us human. What is freedom of expressio

Without the freedom to offend, it ceases to exist. Without the freedom to

enge, even to satirise all orthodoxies, including religious orthodoxies, i

eases to exist. Language and the imagination cannot be imprisoned, o

ression? Without the freedom to offend, it ceases to exist.

s freedom of expression? Without the freedom to offend, it ceas

Vithout the freedom to challenge, even to satirise all orthodoxies, inclu

eligious orthodoxies, it ceases to exist. Language and the imagina

annot be imprisoned, or art will die, and with it, a littl

hat makes us human. What is freedom of

expression? Without the freedom to offend, it ceases to e

Vithout the freedom to challenge, even to satirise all orthodoxies, inclu

eligious orthodoxies, it ce

e imprisoned, or art will die, and with it, a little of what makes us hun

s *freedom of expression? Without the freedom to offend, it ceases to*

om to challenge, even to satirise all orthodoxies, in-

g religious orthodoxies, it ceases to exist.

CENSORING *the word*

Without the freedom to challenge, even to satirise all orthodox

luding religious orthodoxies, it ceases to exist. Language and the

ation cannot be imprisoned, or art will die, and with it, a little of wha

us human. What is freedom of expression? Without the freedom to of-

ceases to exist. Without the freedom to challenge, even to satirise all

ous orthodoxies, it ceases to exist. Language and

akes us human. What is freedom of expression? Without the

dom to offend, it ceases to exist. *Without the*

n to challenge, even to satirise all orthodoxies, including religious or-

xist. JULIAN PETLEY

What is

n of expression? Without the freedom to offend, it est. *With-*

freedom to challenge, even to satir

ithout the freedom to challenge, even to satirise all orthodoxies, in-

uage and the imagina-

not be impris *it, a little of what makes*

an. What is freedom of expression? Without the freedom to offend, it

to exist. Without the freedom to challenge, even to satirise all orthodox

luding religious orthodoxies,

and with it, a little of wha

us human. What is

Seagull
BOOKS
LONDON NEW YORK CALCUTTA

ceases to exist. Without the freedom to challenge, even to satirise all

guage and

Seagull Books

Editorial offices:

1st Floor, Angel Court, 81 St Clements Street
Oxford OX4 1AW, UK

1 Washington Square Village, Apt 1U
New York, NY 10012, USA

26 Circus Avenue, Calcutta 700 017, India

ISBN-10   1 90542 254 7
ISBN-13   978 1 90542 254 8

British Library Cataloguing-in-Publication Data
A catalogue record for this book is available
from the British Library

Typeset and designed by Seagull Books, Calcutta, India
Printed and bound in the United Kingdom
by Biddles Ltd, King's Lynn

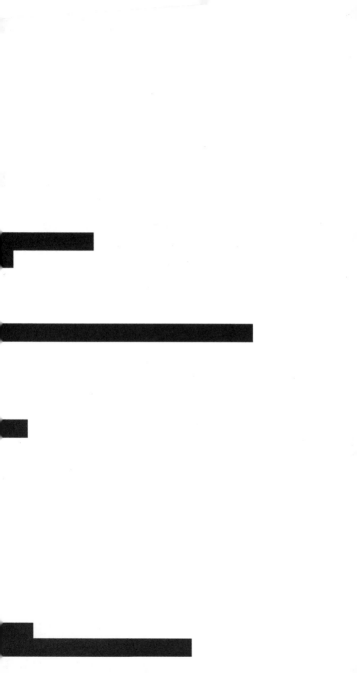

What is freedom of expression? Without the freedom to offend, it ceases to exist. Without the freedom to challenge, even to satirise all orthodoxies, including religious orthodoxies, it ceases to exist. Language and the imagination cannot be imprisoned, or art will die, and with it, a little of what makes us human.

Salman Rushdie, *Imaginary Homelands*

HOW CENSORSHIP WORKS

On the Freedom Forum memorial in Arlington, Virginia, are inscribed the names of 1,700 journalists. In the past 10 years, over 1,000 newsgathering personnel have been killed in the course of doing their jobs—that works out at two per week. In 2006 alone, 137 journalists and 30 other newsgathering personnel were killed, making it the worst year on record for news media fatalities.

Most of these died in their own countries, reporting on local conflicts, corruption and other forms of crime. Iraq was the worst killing field with 68 deaths—all but two Iraqi—bringing the total number of news media lives claimed since the start of the war in 2003 to 169. Outside Iraq, the worst countries for such deaths were the Phillipines (15), Mexico (eight), Sri Lanka (seven) and Guyana (six). A particularly prominent casualty was Anna Politkovskaia, the special correspondent for the Russian independent newspaper *Novaya Gazeta*, who was well known for her investigative reports on corruption and human rights abuses, not least in Chechnya.

Killing journalists—and indeed anyone involved in communicating ideas to others —is undoubtedly the most direct and most brutal form of censorship.

On 10 May 1933, members of the SA and Nazi youth groups publicly burned around 20,000 books in front of the University of Berlin. Authors included Karl Marx, Sigmund Freud, Thomas and Heinrich Mann, Maxim Gorky, Henri Barbusse, Arnold and Stefan Zweig, Havelock Ellis, Marcel Proust, Albert Einstein, Jack London, Upton Sinclair, H. G. Wells and Heinrich Heine. This last had all too presciently observed in 1823 that 'wherever they burn books, they will end up burning people'. This is a method of censorship

Anna Politkovskaia, the special correspondent for the
Russian independent newspaper *Novaya Gazeta*.

Through Light to Night. Thus spake Dr Goebbels: let us new fires make, so the blinded don't awake. From *Arbeiter-Illustrierte-Zeitung*, 10 May 1933.

which is potently symbolic, and it has a
long—and, sadly, ongoing—history,
stretching from China's Qin Dynasty c.213
BC, when dissenting scholars were also
buried alive, through Savonarola's 'Bonfire
of the Vanities' in 1497, the widespread
burnings of the works of Martin Luther and
of Bibles published in the vernacular in six-
teenth-century Europe, the destruction of
Salman Rushdie's *The Satanic Verses* in
Bolton and Bradford, England, in 1988
and 1989 respectively, and the firebombing
of two bookshops in Berkeley, California,
which had the temerity to stock it, to, most
recently, church-organized burnings of the
Harry Potter books in various US cities.

Many of the books burned by the
Roman Catholic church in previous
centuries have featured on one of their
various Indexes, the most famous example
of which is the *Index Librorum Prohibitorum*
established by Pope Paul IV in 1559. In

more recent times, the Soviet Union, Nazi Germany, the Greek dictatorship (1967–74) and the apartheid regime of South Africa have all produced similar lists. These are a potent form of censorship that serves as a clear warning to publishers, booksellers and readers that certain texts are taboo, and that to be found in possession of them may result in forms of extremely severe punishment, including death.

The original *Index* listed around 550 authors including Boccaccio, Rabelais, Erasmus and Machiavelli in an attempt to 'expunge from human memory the names of heretics'. In 1564, Pope Pius IV published the *Tridentine Index*, which forbade all books published by heretics since 1515, unauthorized editions of the Bible, obscene works and books of superstition. These proscriptions remained in effect, with modifications, for three centuries. In 1593, Pope Clement VII required printers to send a copy of every new book to the Congregation of the Index so that it could receive their seal of approval, the *testamur* (later *imprimatur*). Pope Alexander VII's *Index* of 1664 added to the list of works by Copernicus, Galileo, Bacon, Descartes, Hobbes, Pascal, Spinoza and Locke, while that of Benedict XIV in 1758 included many of the great names among thinkers and writers of the Enlightenment, among them Berkeley, Diderot, Hume, Kant, Montesquieu, Rousseau, Gibbon, Defoe, Goldsmith, Richardson and Sterne.

Changing standards of taste in the nineteenth century served to swell the list even further, adding works by Comte, Flaubert, Balzac, Dumas (father and son), Stendhal, Heine, Hugo, Zola and Mill. Indeed, by 1881, no less than 4,000 books were listed. At this point, Pope Leo XIII lifted bans on pre-seventeenth-century writings, Bibles edited by non-Catholics and obscene works by classical authors, although works containing the 'great evil' of heresy, obscene books by non-classical authors, attacks on Catholicism and works that condoned suicide, divorce and duelling remained on the list. However, the final edition of the *Index*, published in 1948, still contained over 4,000 books, including works by Balzac, Descartes, Hobbes, Hume and Voltaire, with new additions by Bergson, Croce, France and Sartre. The *Index* was finally abolished in 1966.

Banning works once they have been published can be difficult and, often, extremely counter-productive. Better, then, to prevent troublesome publications from appearing in the first place. One of the most effective means of doing this in the era of the printed word was by licensing printers and publishers. In Britain, such a licensing system was established by Royal Charter in 1557 which gave a printing monopoly to members of the Stationers' Company. Though basically a trade organization, this worked closely with church and state to track down and have punished, often brutally, unlicensed printers, and expelled those of its own members who published material deemed seditious. Its power was further increased in 1586 by a Decree for Order in Printing which was issued by the much-feared Court of the Star Chamber and which, in an effort to root out clandestine presses, laid down that printing must be confined to London, Oxford and Cambridge. The Star Chamber was abolished in 1641 by Cromwell's republican revolution, and with it licensing of the press, but the latter all too soon returned, occasioning John Milton to write his impassioned defence of freedom of expression, the *Areopagitica*, in 1644 (see below). And two years after the Restoration, in 1660, came the Licensing Act which returned to the Stationers' Company all its previous powers. The number of London printers was reduced to 20, only four foundries were licensed to cast type and all master printers and founders had to post a £300 surety against transgression. As Robert Hargreaves explains:

> The act forbade the publication of any book or pamphlet unless it was first 'lawfully authorised' according to its category. History books, for instance, were to be licensed by the Secretary of State, works of philosophy or science by the Church. Book-sellers and even street hawkers were forced to post bonds, while pamphlets and other ephemeral works were placed under an official surveyor of the press, Roger L' Estrange, who was given a monopoly of printing news and empowered to destroy and deface the equipment of his unlicensed rivals (2002: 102).

In 1695, the licensing system was abolished for the printed word. However, this was mainly because the Stationers' Company had blatantly abused its monopoly over patents and copyrights and had thus brought the Act into disrepute. Furthermore, with printing becoming ever easier and cheaper, the licensing system was becoming increasingly difficult to police. On the other hand, the courts had already begun to find new means of discouraging freedom of expression, in the form of prosecutions for blasphemy, sedition and criminal libel.

Meanwhile, another form of licensing, theatre censorship, which had been in the hands of the Master of the Revels since at least the mid-sixteenth century, was passed to another member of the Royal Household, the Lord Chamberlain, by the Licensing Act of 1737. From then, until as late as 1968, only plays which he had approved in advance could be performed in public. This was a draconian and entirely unaccountable system of censorship. As Nicholas De Jongh puts it:

> The processes by which the Chamberlain's Examiner of Plays worked were rarely disclosed and his reasons for censoring plays or cutting scenes, incidents or words were not publicly divulged. All the Chamberlain's or Examiner's communications with theatre producers who sought to present plays, or theatre managers responsible for selecting plays for particular theatres, were regarded as confidential. The Lord Chamberlain's judgement was final and he would not enter into discussion with playwrights. There was no court of appeal and no questions about his decisions could be tabled in the House of Commons or the Lords (2000: ix–x).

During the Lord Chamberlain's 230-year reign, countless plays were subject to cuts, and various major works banned outright. These included Shaw's *Mrs Warren's Profession*, Ibsen's *Ghosts*, Pirandello's *Six Characters in Search of an Author*, Tolstoy's *Power of Darkness*, Granville Barker's *Waste*, Beckett's *Endgame* and Osborne's *A Patriot for Me*.

Such forms of licensing may today seem archaic and anachronistic, but are, in fact, not so very different from the certificates handed out by the British Board of Film Classification (BBFC) in the UK and the Motion Picture Association (MPAA) in the US. In both countries most cinemas would be highly unlikely to show movies without such seals of approval, the granting of which may well depend upon cutting of certain scenes; furthermore, in the UK it is actually illegal to distribute, sell or rent movies on video or DVD without a BBFC certificate, which, in the case of these forms of dissemination, has statutory force.

Another, more modern, form of censorship consists in attempting to price problematic works out of the marketplace. Here again the history of the British press furnishes a useful example.

In the nineteenth century, the authorities found the laws on seditious and blasphemous libel increasingly difficult to enforce. Juries were often reluctant to convict, and defendants were good at casting themselves in the role of martyrs in the cause of free speech. Thus there were only 16 prosecutions for seditious and blasphemous libel from 1825 to 1834 compared with 167 in the preceding eight years. As a result, as James Curran explains:

> (T)he authorities came to rely increasingly on the newspaper stamp duty and taxes on paper and advertisements as a way of curbing the radical press.

The intention of these press taxes was twofold: to restrict the readership of newspapers to the well-to-do by raising cover prices; and to limit the owner-ship of newspapers to the propertied classes by increasing publishing costs (Curran and Seaton 2003: 7).

Stamp duty had first been introduced in 1712. By 1815 it had increased by 800 per cent, increasing by 266 per cent be-tween 1789 and 1815 alone. In addition, the surety system was re-introduced, with publishers having to place bonds of be-tween £200 and £300 with the authorities. These measures did, indeed, weaken the radical press for a while, but it revived in the 1830s, partly because of renewed social unrest but also because it went under-ground and evaded the stamp duty. Be-tween 1830 and 1836, some 800 publishers and sellers of unstamped newspapers were imprisoned, but the radical press continued to flourish. The Whig government responded in 1836 with a two-pronged attack: it brought in new measures which strengthened the government's search-and-destroy powers and it reduced the stamp duty by 75 per cent.

These measures had two consequences. First, radical newspapers were forced to pay stamp duty, and thus had to increase their prices. To some extent, the price rises were offset by groups of working people pooling their resources in order to buy radical papers. But, second, they encouraged, exactly as they were designed to do, men of capital, convinced anti-radicals, to invest in the newspaper market and so compete with the radical press both economically and ideologically. It was largely this motive that lay behind the abolition of advertisement duty in 1853, the stamp duty in 1855, the paper duty in 1861 and the surety system in 1869.

Monopoly Money. By permission of the Campaign for Press and Broadcasting Freedom.

With powerful capitalist forces entering the newspaper market, considerable technological innovation and development followed. Increasingly, a craft system of newspaper production was replaced by an industrial one. This had the result of significantly increasing both running costs and fixed capital costs in the newspaper sector, making it difficult for those with more limited funds to remain in, let alone break into, the marketplace. On the other hand, the major operators could benefit from economies of scale, offering attractive products while still keeping cover prices low. The combination of rising expenditure and lower cover prices forced up the circulation levels newspapers needed to reach in order to become profitable. This, in turn, made it more difficult for new entrants to join the marketplace, especially if they were undercapitalized and not aimed at a mass audience. Thus, as Curran rightly concludes:

Market forces accomplished more than the most repressive measures of an aristocratic state. The security system introduced in 1819 to ensure that the press was controlled by 'men of some respectability and capital' had fixed the financial qualifications of press ownership at a mere £200 to £300. This financial hurdle was raised over a hundredfold by the market system between 1850 and 1920 (ibid.: 29).

Equally significant in marginalizing (and ultimately destroying) the radical press was the rise of advertising as a means of funding newspapers after the abolition of the advertisement duty in 1853. The influx of advertising revenue meant that newspapers could halve their cover prices, and then halve them again, in subsequent decades. But it also meant that they became heavily dependent on advertising, as their net cover prices no longer covered their costs. As Curran puts it: 'Advertisers thus acquired a *de facto* licensing power because, without their support, newspapers ceased to be economically viable' (ibid.: 30).

Radical newspapers were unattractive to many advertisers for two reasons—their politics and the nature of their readership. On the latter point, the head of a well-known advertising agency wrote in 1856: 'Some of the most widely circulated journals in the Empire are the worst possible to advertise in. Their readers are not purchasers, and any money thrown upon them is so much thrown away', while in 1921, an advertising handbook warned: 'You cannot afford to place your advertisements in a paper which is read by the down-at-heels who buy it to see the "Situations Vacant" column' (both quoted in ibid.: 31). Radical papers were left with two options—either to move upmarket in an effort to attract the kind of readers attractive to advertisers or to remain minority publications with manageable losses that could be offset by donations from readers. What they could not do, without incurring crippling losses, was to move into the mass market and sell themselves, without advertising, as cheaply as competitors effectively subsidized by the advertisers.

This brings us to considering market forces and commercial pressures as agents of censorship. Although these are generally regarded as relatively recent developments, the *Areopagitica* actually contains a warning that freedom of expression can be confined by commercial forces as well as political or religious ones. Thus:

> Truth and understanding are not such wares as to be monopolised and traded in by tickets and statutes and standards. We must not think how to make a staple commodity of all the knowledge in the land, to mark it and license it like

our broadcloth and our woolpacks
(Milton 1990: 600–1).

In recent times, with the growth of huge,
global, cross-media oligopolies and the rap-
idly increasing commodification of culture
and information of all kinds, such a warning
seems particularly premonitory. It was
echoed in 1991 by John Keane in *The Media
and Democracy*, a book which reads as ever
more timely, in which he argues that those
concerned with freedom of expression in the
contemporary media must realize that:

> Communications markets restrict free-
> dom of communication by generating
> barriers to entry, monopoly and restric-
> tions upon choice, and by shifting the
> prevailing definition of information
> from that of a public good to a privately
> appropriable commodity. In short, it
> must be concluded that there is a struc-
> tural contradiction between freedom of
> communication and unlimited freedom

of the market, and that the liberal market ideology of freedom of individual choice in the marketplace of opinions is in fact a justification for the privileging of corporate speech and of giving more choice to investors than to citizens. It is an apology for the power of king-sized business to organise and determine and, therefore, to *censor* individuals' choices concerning what they listen to or read and watch . . . Market competition produces market censorship. Private ownership of the media produces private caprice. Those who control the market sphere of producing and distributing information determine, prior to publication, what products (such as books, magazines, newspapers, television programmes, computer software) will be mass produced and, thus, which opinions officially gain entry into the 'marketplace of opinions' (1991: 90).

A Steve Bell cartoon from 1994 for the Campaign for Press and Broadcasting Freedom.

We shall return to these points in greater detail later.

FREEDOM OF EXPRESSION

In this introductory survey of the main forms of censorship, it has been taken for granted that freedom of expression is a 'good thing'. However, by no means everybody, either in the West or elsewhere, would go along with such an assumption. We therefore need to explore the main arguments that have been put forward for protecting freedom of expression and, in particular, to enquire whether the 'classic' arguments still hold good today in circumstances very different from those in which they were first advanced.

Freedom of expression, whether for individuals or the media, is generally thought of as one of the defining features of a democracy. It is endorsed in ringing tones in the First Amendment of the US Constitution, which states that:

> Congress shall make no law respecting an establishment of religion, or prohibiting the free exercise thereof; or abridging the freedom of speech or of the press.

In the same year, 1789, that the Constitution took effect, in France the 'Declaration of the Rights of Man and the Citizen' laid down that:

> No one is to be disquieted because of his opinions . . . Free communication of ideas and opinions is one of the most precious of the rights of man.

Later, in the wake of the terrible shock to civilization that was World War II, the United Nations was founded, and Article 19 of its Universal Declaration of Human Rights (1948) declared that:

> Everyone has the right to freedom of
> opinion and expression; this right in-
> cludes freedom to hold opinions with-
> out interference and to seek, receive
> and impart information and ideas
> through any media and regardless of
> frontiers.

Virtually identical sentiments may be
found in the European Convention on
Human Rights (1953). In 1976, the European Court of Human Rights laid down a
particularly powerful defence of this principle when it ruled that:

> Freedom of expression constitutes one
> of the essential foundations of a demo-
> cratic society and one of the basic condi-
> tions for its progress and for each
> individual's self-fulfilment. It is applica-
> ble not only to information or ideas
> that are favourably received or re-
> garded as inoffensive or as a matter of
> indifference, but also to those that

offend, shock or disturb. Such are the
demands of pluralism, tolerance and
broad-mindedness without which there
is no democratic society (quoted in
Robertson and Nicol 2002: 37).

However, this is not to say that freedom of expression is or should be absolute. Particularly in times of war, it may
be necessary to suppress certain kinds of
information on the grounds of national
security, and few would want to defend the
production and distribution of images that
record actual rapes and instances of child
abuse, for example. All democratic countries possess laws that curtail media freedom in one way or another (the UK has
over 60), and the situation was concisely
summed up by its Law Lords in 1936 when
they stated that:

Free speech does not mean free
speech; it means speech hedged in by
all the laws against blasphemy, sedition

and so forth. It means freedom governed by law (quoted in ibid.: 2).

Within individual democratic countries
the degree of freedom of expression
granted to different media frequently
varies: some democratic countries are more
liberal than others in matters of freedom of
expression. For example, freedom of expression in the US is constitutionally pro-
tected while in the UK, which lacks a
written constitution, it is not.

FREEDOM OF SPEECH AND FREEDOM OF THE MEDIA

It is worth noting that the US Constitution
actually makes a distinction between freedom of speech and freedom of the press: in
other words, between individual and mediated communication. As we shall see later,
this raises interesting questions about

whether the same defences can or should be applied to both. A related point in the case of the media is that the meaning of the phrase 'freedom of expression' may vary considerably according to one's place in the process of media production, distribution and consumption. For example, for media proprietors, freedom of expression may mean the freedom to own media and the freedom to use those media to express their own ideas and to further their own business interests; it will probably also include freedom from interference by government in the form of censorship or ownership regulation and, quite possibly, freedom from trade union organization. Meanwhile, for their employees, freedom of expression may mean the freedom to exercise professional autonomy, which will include not only freedom from censorship but also from the dictates of proprietors, managers and advertisers. It may well also entail the freedom to follow the dictates of their own conscience in their work and the freedom to join a union and to obey its codes of conduct. Finally, for the media consumer, media freedom may include the freedom to access a wide range of different kinds of material and a plurality of viewpoints, as well as the possibility of making their own voice heard in the media. It may also include freedom from intrusion by the media and freedom from media content they find offensive.

From these considerations, it can readily be grasped that freedom of expression, when applied to the media, means a great deal more than those owning or working in the media being free from censorship and other forms of content regulation. In particular, we have to recognize that regulation and freedom are not necessarily inimical one to another, and that certain forms of media regulation—such as those intended to ensure diversity and plurality, and to discourage oligopoly and the abuse of proprietor-power—may, indeed, enhance freedom of expression in the full sense of the term. For example, the principles of public service broadcasting, which attempt to ensure that, *inter alia*, news and current affairs programmes are presented in an impartial way, that a balance is struck between information and entertainment, and that minority tastes, views and communities are adequately catered for, may, in the strict sense of the term, be forms of regulation, but in no way can they be considered forms of censorship.

Although most people in the West and in other significant democracies around the world today take the importance of freedom of expression for granted, this is, in fact, a relatively recent notion. Its beginnings lie in the development of printing in the fifteenth century and, in particular, in

Reformation struggles to make the Bible and other religious texts available in the vernacular. It was further boosted by the growth of rationality and literacy, and emerged in the eighteenth century as a central value of the European Enlightenment, with its basic premise that the truth was capable of discovery and demonstration, and that there was no longer any need for deference to traditional authorities and outdated dogmas.

'BOOKS PROMISCUOUSLY READ'

However, one of the greatest defences of freedom of expression, the *Areopagitica*, published in 1644, actually preceded the Enlightenment by over a century. Subtitled 'A Speech of Mr John Milton for the Liberty of Unlicensed Printing', this was Milton's impassioned protest against the Licensing Order passed by the English

Parliament in June 1643, which effectively
revived one of the more oppressive measures of the previous monarchy, namely the
banning of all publishers and publications
not licensed by the state.

The *Areopagitica* is obviously of its time,
not least in its frequent invocations of God.
Nonetheless, many of its defences of freedom of expression ring as true today as
when they were written. For example, the
notion that ideas need to be constantly
challenged and put to the test, as encapsu-
lated in one of Milton's most famous
remarks:

> I cannot praise a fugitive and cloistered
> virtue, unexercised and unbreathed,
> that never sallies out and sees her ad-
> versary, but slinks out of the race,
> where that immortal garland is to be
> run for, not without dust and heat. As-
> suredly we bring not innocence into the
> world, we bring impurity much rather;

that which purifies us is trial, and trial
is by what is contrary (1990: 590).

Milton also mounts a strong defence of
new, and thus quite probably unpopular,
ideas when he states that:

> If it come to prohibiting, there is not
> aught more likely to be prohibited than
> truth itself; whose first appearance to our
> eyes, bleared and dimmed with prejudice
> and custom, is more unsightly and un-
> plausible than many errors (ibid.: 615).

Similarly, he extends the defence to
ideas which some may find distasteful or
unpleasant in his argument that:

> Bad meat will scarce breed good nourish-
> ment in the healthiest concoction; but
> herein the difference is of bad books,
> that they to a discreet and judicious
> reader serve in many ways to discover, to
> confute, to forewarn and to illustrate
> (ibid.: 588).

This leads him to conclude that:

> Since therefore the knowledge and survey of vice is in this world so necessary to the constituting of human virtue, and the scanning of error to the confirmation of truth, how can we more safely, and with less danger, scout into the regions of sin and falsity than by reading all manner of tractates and hearing all manner of reason. And this is the benefit which may be had of books promiscuously read (ibid.: 590).

In Milton's view, people were perfectly capable of distinguishing right from wrong, good from bad, by the exercise of their reason and, in order to exercise that faculty, should have unlimited access to the ideas and thoughts of others. Truth would survive because it was true and thus should be able to assert itself against error and falsehood. As he put it: 'Let her [Truth] and Falsehood grapple; who ever knew Truth

put to the worse, in a free and open encounter?' (Ibid.: 613.) For him, the written
word played a key role in what was essentially a self-righting process:

> As good almost kill a man as kill a good
> book: who kills a man kills a reasonable
> creature, God's image; but he who de-
> stroys a good book, kills reason itself, kills
> the image of God, as it were in the eye
> (ibid.: 578).

'THIS FORMIDABLE CENSOR
OF THE PUBLIC FUNCTIONARIES'

If, in Milton, we find one of the first state-
ments of the idea that freedom of expression
is crucial if people are to be able to understand the truth, then in David Hume's 1741
essay 'Of the Liberty of the Press' we encounter an early version of the notion that it
is necessary in order to ward off despotism:

Arbitrary power would steal in upon us,
were we not careful to prevent its
progress, and were there not an easy
method of conveying the alarm from
one end of the kingdom to the other.
The spirit of the people must frequently
be roused, in order to curb the ambition
of the court; and the dread of rousing
this spirit must be employed to prevent
that ambition. Nothing is so effectual to
this purpose as the liberty of the press,
by which all the learning, wit, and ge-
nius of the nation may be employed on
the side of freedom, and every one be
animated to its defence (1994: 100).

In the works of Tom Paine, we find
both ideas combined: namely, that it is by
people exercising their reason, via a free
press, that governments are most effectively
prevented from abusing their authority. But
it is actually in the great speech made on 18
December 1792 by Thomas Erskine at

Paine's trial on a charge of seditious libel
that we find the clearest expression of this
particular point of view:

> The proposition which I mean to main-
> tain as the basis of the liberty of the
> press, and without which it is an empty
> sound, is this:—that every man, not in-
> tending to mislead, but seeking to en-
> lighten others with what his own reading
> and conscience, however erroneously,
> have dictated to him as truth, may ad-
> dress himself to the universal reason of a
> whole nation, either upon the subject of
> government in general, or upon that of
> our own particular country:—that he may
> analyse the principles of its constitu-
> tion,—point out its errors and defects,—
> examine and publish its corruptions,
> —warn his fellow citizens against their
> ruinous consequences,—and exert his
> whole faculties in pointing out the most
> advantageous changes in establishments

which he considers to be radically defec-
tive, or sliding from their object by abuse
. . . In this manner power has reasoned
in every age: government, in *its own esti-
mation*, has been *at all times* a system of
perfection; but a free press has examined
and detected its errors, and the people
have from time to time reformed them.
This freedom has alone made our government what it is; this freedom alone
can preserve it; and therefore, under the
banner of that freedom, today I stand up
to defend Thomas Paine (quoted in
Williamson 1973: 189).

Paine was a major influence on Thomas
Jefferson, who drafted the 1776 Declaration
of Independence and was US President from
1801 to 1809. For Jefferson, the press was an
essential source of information and guid-
ance, and a free press was absolutely necessary if citizens were to perform their full role
in a democracy. As he put it in 1804:

No experiment can be more interesting
than that we are now trying, and which
we trust will end in establishing the
fact, that man may be governed by reason and truth. Our first object should
therefore be, to leave open to him all
avenues to truth. The most effectual
hitherto found, is the freedom of the
press. It is therefore the first shut up by
those who fear the investigation of their
actions. The firmness with which the
people have withstood the late abuses
of the press, the discernment they have
manifested between truth and falsehood, show that they may safely be
trusted to hear everything true and
false, and to form a correct judgement
between them (1993: 527).

Much later, in 1823, Jefferson, who by
this time was himself no stranger to newspaper hostility, described the press as 'this
formidable censor of the public functionar-

ies [which,] by arraigning them at the tribunal of public opinion, produces reform peaceably, which must otherwise be done by revolution', and as 'the best instrument for enlarging the mind of man, and improving him as a rational, moral, and social being' (quoted in Mayer 1994: 181). In Jefferson's view, governments that cannot stand up to criticism deserve to fall; for him, the strength of a government lay precisely in its willingness to permit criticism and its ability to withstand it. As he had put it in 1792:

> No government ought to be without censors; and where the press is free, no one ever will. If virtuous, it need not fear the fair operation of attack and defence. Nature has given to man no other means of sifting out the truth either in religion, law or politics (quoted in ibid.: 173).

Indeed, in 1787, Jefferson had gone so far as to state that:

> The basis of our government being the opinion of the people, the first object should be to keep that right; and were it left to me to decide whether we should have a government without newspapers or newspapers without government, I should not hesitate to prefer the latter. But I should mean that every man should receive these papers, and be capable of reading them (1993: 381).

The final sentence is often omitted from this famous quote, but it is essential to Jefferson's point, which maintains that freedom of expression is not simply a matter of publishers' right to publish but also requires universal literacy and universal rights of access to published material. We shall return to this point later.

Jefferson's ideas have been immensely influential in the US. For example, their echo can be clearly heard in Justice Louis Brandeis' famous 1927 judgement in the case of *Whitney v. California*:

> Those who won our independence believed that the final end of the State was to make men free to develop their faculties; and that in its government the deliberative forces should prevail over the arbitrary . . . They believed that freedom to think as you will and to speak as you think are means indispensable to the discovery and spread of political truth . . . that the greatest menace to freedom is an inert people; that public discussion is a political duty; and that this should be a fundamental principle of American government (quoted in Barendt 2005: 18).

LIBERTY AND TRUTH

In the UK, on the other hand, it is John
Stuart Mill's ideas on freedom that have
tended to predominate. For Mill, in *On
Liberty*, freedom of expression is key among
the liberties which 'to a considerable
amount form part of the political morality
of all countries which profess religious tol-
eration and free institutions' (1985: 73). He
defines liberty as the right of the individual
to think and act as they wish, providing that
they harm no one else by doing so, arguing
that:

> The only purpose for which power can
> be rightfully exercised over any mem-
> ber of a civilised community, against
> his will, is to prevent harm to others
> (ibid.: 68).

For Mill, 'all silencing of discussion is
an assumption of infallibility' (ibid.: 77).
Enlarging on what he means by 'infallibility' in this context, he explains: 'It is not the

feeling sure of a doctrine (be it what it may)
which I call an assumption of infallibility. It
is the undertaking to decide that question
for others, without allowing them to hear
what can be said on the contrary side' (ibid.:
83). He later summarizes his four major arguments for freedom of expression thus:

> First, if any opinion is compelled to si-
> lence, that opinion may, for aught we
> can certainly know, be true. To deny
> this is to assume our own infallibility.
>
> Secondly, though the silenced
> opinion be an error, it may, and very
> commonly does, contain a portion of
> truth; and since the general or prevail-
> ing opinion on any subject is rarely or
> never the whole truth, it is only by a
> collision of adverse opinions that the
> remainder of the truth has any chance
> of being supplied.
>
> Thirdly, even if the received opin-
> ion be not only true, but the whole

truth; unless it is suffered to be, and actually is, vigorously and earnestly con-
tested, it will, by most of those who
receive it, be held in the manner of a
prejudice, with little comprehension or
feeling of its rational grounds. And not
only this, but, fourthly, the meaning of
the doctrine itself will be in danger of
being lost or enfeebled, and deprived
of its vital effect on the character and
conduct: the dogma becoming a mere
formal profession, inefficacious for
good, but cumbering the ground and
preventing the growth of any real and
heartfelt conviction from reason or personal experience (ibid.: 115–16).

In other words, if we silence what we
take to be mere opinion we may be silencing the truth; a wrong opinion may contain
a grain of truth necessary for finding the
whole truth; opinions, even true ones, tend
to become prejudices over time if not ar-

gued over and defended; and uncontested opinions lose their vitality and effectiveness. And, like Milton, Mill was a stout defender of unpopular and minority views, as in this justly famous passage:

> If all mankind minus one were of one opinion, mankind would be no more justified in silencing that one person than he, if he had the power, would be justified in silencing mankind. Were an opinion a personal possession of no value except to the owner, if to be obstructed in the enjoyment of it were simply a private injury, it would make some difference whether the injury was inflicted only on a few persons or on many. But the peculiar evil of silencing the expression of an opinion is that it is robbing the human race, posterity as well as the existing generation—those who dissent from the opinion, still more those who hold it. If the opinion is right,

they are deprived of the opportunity of exchanging error for truth; if wrong, they lose, what is almost as great a benefit, the clearer perception and livelier impression of truth produced by its collision with error (ibid.: 76).

LIBERTY, LICENCE AND LIBEL

However, as noted earlier, few would defend freedom of expression in absolute terms, and these classical exponents of the principle were no exceptions. Thus, for example, Milton's tolerance did not extend to

Popery and open superstition, which, as it extirpates all religious and civil supremacies, should itself be extirpated, provided first that all charitable and compassionate means be used to win and regain the weak and misled: that also which is impious or evil absolutely

either against faith or manner no law
can possibly permit, that intends not to
unlaw itself (1990: 615).

He also argued that the Common-
wealth should 'have a vigilant eye how
books demean themselves as well as men;
and thereafter to confine, imprison and do
sharpest justice on them as malefactors'
(ibid.: 578). As Christopher Hill points out,
Milton specifically excluded Roman
Catholics from being allowed to express
themselves freely because he regarded
Roman Catholicism as idolatry, one of the
most grievous sins described in the Bible,
and thus not so much a religion as a
'priestly despotism under the cloak of religion . . . a "Roman principality", the out-
ward arm of the Italian potentates whom he
regarded as Antichrist, leader of a potential
Spanish or French fifth column in England'
(1977: 55).

For Tom Paine, meanwhile, privately owned newspapers were a 'public matter', and there was a significant difference for him between the exercise of editorial power and the liberty of the press. As he stated in 1786, after the *Pennsylvania Packet* refused to publish several of his articles:

> If the freedom of the press is to be determined by the judgement of the printer of a Newspaper in preference to that of the people, who when they read will judge for themselves, the[n] freedom is on a very sandy foundation' (quoted in Keane 1996: 262).

Paine clearly believed that liberty of the press was not equivalent to liberty to libel, and that the distinction ought to be legally recognized and enforced. Later, in his 1806 essay 'Liberty of the Press', Paine complained that:

Nothing is more common with printers,
especially of newspapers, than the con-
tinual cry of the Liberty of the Press, as if
because they are printers they are to
have more privileges than other people
. . . A man does not ask liberty before-
hand to say something he has a mind
to say but he becomes answerable after-
wards for the atrocities he may utter. In
like manner, if a man makes the press
utter atrocious things, he becomes as answerable for them as if he had uttered
them by word of mouth.

The term 'free press' thus refers to 'the
fact of printing free from prior restraint,
and not at all to the matter printed,
whether good or bad. The public at large
or in the case of prosecution, a jury of the
county—will be the judges of the matter.' In
this respect, the radical Paine's view is identical to that of the conservative William
Blackstone in his *Commentaries on the Laws of*

England (1765), a view that is generally taken to mean that it is prior restraint of the media, not post-publication censure of it, which is generally incompatible with the principle of freedom of expression:

> The liberty of the press is indeed essential to the nature of a free state; but this consists in laying no previous restraints on publications, and not in freedom from censure for criminal matter when published. Every free man has an undoubted right to lay what sentiments he pleases before the public; to forbid this is to destroy the freedom of the press; but if he publishes what is improper, mischievous or illegal, he must take the consequences of his own temerity (quoted in Robertson and Nicol 2002: 19).

Paine's comments indicate that even as early as the late-eighteenth century, the now common argument that freedom of expression and freedom of the press are simply synonymous had already taken firm hold in publishing circles. This impression is reinforced by the fact that in 1789, Benjamin Franklin made the ironic comment that:

> My proposal then is to leave the liberty of the press untouched, to be exercised in its full extent, force, and vigour; but to permit the *liberty of the cudgel* to go with it *pari passu*. Thus, my fellow citizens, if an impudent writer attacks your reputation, dearer to you perhaps than your life, and puts your name to the charge, you may go to him as openly and break his head (quoted in Holmes 1990: 37).

By the start of the following century, Thomas Jefferson himself had become the object of considerable hostility from the Federal press. In the course of his Second Inaugural Address on 4 March 1805, he noted that:

During this course of administration, and in order to disturb it, the artillery of the press has been levelled against us, charged us with whatsoever its licentiousness could devise or dare. These abuses of an institution so important to freedom and science are deeply to be regretted inasmuch as they tend to lessen its usefulness, and to sap its safety.

Suggesting that only the demands of more important matters had prevented several States from invoking their laws forbidding falsehood and defamation, Jefferson added that:

No inference is here intended, that the laws, provided by the State against false and defamatory publications, should not be enforced; he who has time, renders a service to public morals and public tranquillity, in reforming these abuses by the salutary coercions of the law (1993: 316–17).

In other words, the freedom of the press to publish did not, in his view, include freedom from prosecution for spreading untruths and perpetrating libels.

We have already seen that Mill's philosophy of freedom allowed for the prevention of activities that harm others. To illustrate how this works in the area of expression, Milton provided a now well-known example:

> Even opinions lose their immunity when the circumstances in which they are expressed are such as to constitute their expression a positive instigation to some mischievous act. An opinion that corn dealers are starvers of the poor, or that private property is robbery, ought to be unmolested when simply circulated through the press, but may justly incur punishment when delivered orally to an excited mob assembled before the house of a corn dealer, or when handed about among

True Blue: The Tory Tabloids. By permission of the
Campaign for Press and Broadcasting Freedom.

the same mob in the form of a placard
(1985: 119).

The problem with this formulation,
however, is that 'opinions circulated
through the press' have indeed resulted in
baying and vengeful mobs gathering outside people's houses, most recently, in the
UK, as a result of the *News of the World*'s
campaign to 'name and shame' pae-
dophiles, thus fatally undermining the particular distinction Mill was attempting to
erect. More generally, however, it is not entirely clear what Mill actually *means* by
harm, thus making it the subject of endless
philosophical debate. This would not
matter greatly as long as it served simply as
a means of keeping philosophers happily
employed, but the problem is that a notion
of harm derived from Mill has passed into
UK media law, notably in the case of the
Video Recordings Act which, in the wake of
the murder of James Bulger in 1993 and

amid unfounded allegations that the young killers had been watching violent videos, was amended to require that the BBFC, when censoring or merely classifying works, have 'special regard (among other relevant factors) to any harm that may be caused to potential viewers or, through their behaviour, to society by the manner in which the work deals with (a) criminal behaviour; (b) illegal drugs; (c) violent behaviour or incidents; (d) horrific behaviour or incidents; or (e) human sexual activity'.

At this point, we can no longer avoid asking the obvious, but nonetheless fundamental question: to what extent are the defences of freedom of expression explored above, which were formulated well before the advent of the electronic media, still applicable today?

MILTON, MILL, MURDOCH

Undoubtedly, Milton would have been horrified by much of the contents of the modern media. As Evans argued in 1944, at a conference commemorating the tercentenary of the *Areopagitica*:

> Milton's conception of the circulation of ideas was that which might have prevailed in Greece—a small audience, all of whom are capable of forming their own judgements, with discussion to correct false emphasis. He has in mind the formation of an adequate judgement by a Socratic method. Even the England of his own day did not fit into that picture altogether, and the world of our day does not fit it at all (1944: 28).

Milton could not have foreseen a Rothermere, Beaverbrook, Murdoch or Berlusconi, or, for that matter, a Goebbels or a Stalin, and could he have done so, one very much doubts that he would have de-

Screaming Tabloids. By permission of the Campaign for
Press and Broadcasting Freedom.

fended their varying uses of modern media for propaganda purposes of one kind or another. Nor can we be at all sure that in the modern media landscape, which has variously been described as a hyper-reality, a Tower of Babel and a hall of mirrors, truth will always emerge victorious over falsehood. On the other hand, Milton's defence of rational argument and debate, his championing of new and unpopular ideas, and his recommendation of 'promiscuous reading', along with his warnings about what we would now call market censorship, are as relevant and inspirational today as they were in his lifetime.

Jefferson, as noted earlier, did indeed encounter an early version of the modern press—and deeply disliked it. On the other hand, for all his veiled threats of legal action over falsehood and defamation, Jefferson also argued in his Second Inaugural Address that:

> Since truth and reason have main-
> tained their ground against false opin-
> ions in league with false facts, the
> press, confined to truth, needs no
> other legal restraint; the public judg-
> ment will correct false reasonings and
> opinions, on a full hearing of all par-
> ties; and no other definite line can be
> drawn between the inestimable liberty
> of the press and its demoralising licen-
> tiousness. If there still be impropri-
> eties which this rule would not
> restrain, its supplement must be
> sought in the censorship of public
> opinion (1993: 316–17).

In other words, a press which spread
falsity and licentiousness risked ultimately
the judgement of the marketplace. However, just two years later, in 1805, Jefferson's faith in the court of public opinion
and his confidence in the market to safe-
guard truthful communication seemed to

have waned considerably. Thus, in a letter to John Norvell, he wrote:

> To your request of my opinion of the manner in which a newspaper should be conducted, so as to be most useful, I should answer, 'by restraining it to true facts and sound principles only'. Yet I fear such a paper would find few subscribers. It is a melancholy truth, that a suppression of the press could not more completely deprive the nation of its benefits, than is done by its abandoned prostitution to falsehood. Nothing can now be believed by which is seen in a newspaper. Truth itself becomes suspicious by being put into that polluted vehicle . . . The man who never looks into a newspaper is better informed than he who reads them; inasmuch as he who knows nothing is nearer to truth than he whose mind is filled with falsehoods and errors (ibid.: 533).

He also made the crucial point that those who buy such newspapers also hold a good deal of responsibility for their contents. Thus condemning the 'demoralising practice of feeding the public mind habitually on slander, and the depravity of taste which this nauseous aliment induces', he continues:

> Defamation is becoming a necessary of life; insomuch, that a dish of tea in the morning or evening cannot be digested without this stimulant. Even those who do not believe these abominations, still read them with complaisance to their auditors, and instead of the abhorrence and indignation which should fill a virtuous mind, betray a secret pleasure in the possibility that some may believe them, though they do not themselves. It seems to escape them, that it is not he who prints, but he who pays for printing a slander, who is its real author (ibid.: 533).

Turning now to Mill, one might reasonably ask, without foundering on the wilder shores of postmodernism, whether his arguments for freedom of expression rest on a notion of truth so absolute as now to be problematic. However, Mill does in fact escape this charge. For example, he defines truth as 'so much a question of the reconciling and combining of opposites' (1985: 110) and he also states that:

> Even progress, which ought to superadd, for the most part only substitutes one partial and incomplete truth for another; improvement consisting chiefly in this, that the new fragment of truth is more wanted, more adapted to the needs of the time than that which it displaces (ibid.: 109).

Such sentiments lead Jonathan Riley to conclude that: 'History is viewed by him not as a victorious march of inevitable improvement but rather as a largely cyclical process in which different parts of the truth repeatedly supersede one another, one part setting as another rises' (1998: 66).

A further question is whether defences of freedom of expression based on Mill overestimate the extent to which public discussion today, and in particular the discussion to be found in the modern media, is rational and truth-seeking. Eric Barendt argues that 'Mill's truth argument . . . applies most clearly to speech stating beliefs and theories about political, moral, aesthetic and social matters' (2005: 11), and we return here to one of the problems encountered when trying to apply some of Milton's ideas on freedom of expression in a modern context. Where, for example, do advertising, propaganda, 'spin', press gossip about people's private lives and so on, fit into this rational scheme of things, if at all?

Let us try to answer this question, indirectly at first, by examining a more contemporary defence of freedom of expression—that based on the freedom of the marketplace.

FREEDOM OF EXPRESSION
FOR RUPERT MURDOCH

The notion of the 'marketplace of ideas' first found legal expression in 1919 in the famous dissenting judgement of Mr Justice Holmes in *Abrams v. US*:

> But when men have realised that time has upset many fighting faiths, they may come to believe even more than they believe the very foundations of their own conduct that the ultimate good desired is better reached by free trade in ideas— that the best test of truth is the power of the thought to get itself accepted in the competition of the market, and that truth is the only ground upon which their

wishes can be safely carried out (quoted in ibid.: 11).

Whatever Holmes' intention, this has frequently been taken as a justification for applying 'free market' theory to the realm of communication. According to such theory, the market, left to its own devices, will of itself provide what consumers want, and regulation simply distorts this process. In this neo-liberal view of things ('neo' because this is simply a return to the values of nineteenth-century laissez-faire capitalism), people, viewed as consumers, are best served not by government-regulating companies' economic activities in order to ensure universality and quality of services, but by 'de-regulation': 'freeing' the market and encouraging competition on the part of producers and individual choice on the part of consumers. Here we once again encounter J. S. Mill, who, in his *Principles of Political Economy*, famously argued that:

In all the more advanced communities, the great majority of things are worse done by the intervention of government, than the individuals more interested in the matter would do them, or cause them to be done if left to themselves. The grounds of this truth are expressed with tolerable exactness in the popular dictum, that people understand their own business and their own interests better, and care for them more, than the government does, or can be expected to do. This maxim holds true throughout the greatest part of the business of life, and wherever it is true we ought to condemn every kind of government intervention that conflicts with it (1965: 941–2).

In the UK, ideas such as these greatly animated the Thatcher government that came to power in 1979, and, before long, were being enthusiastically, not to say dogmatically, applied to the broadcasting sector. The press was a medium in which market forces had always been allowed free rein, but hitherto it had been thought that certain forms of provision in society—most notably health, education and broadcasting —were so important to its functioning and cohesion that they could not be left simply to the tender mercies of the market. Such services had to be provided, or at least regulated, by government or other public agencies. Margaret Thatcher and her colleagues had no truck with such interventionist notions and habitually dismissed the BBC and ITV as a 'cosy duopoly'. The Peacock Committee, which Thatcher hoped— quite wrongly, as it turned out—would recommend to her that the BBC should take advertising, and so destroy British public service broadcasting at a stroke, stated in the *Report of the Committee on Financing the BBC* that, provided certain conditions are fulfilled:

> The public are best served if able to buy
> the amount of the service required from
> suppliers who compete for custom
> through price and quality . . . The fun-
> damental aim of broadcasting policy
> should [therefore] be to increase both
> the freedom of choice of the consumer
> and the opportunities available to pro-
> gramme-makers to offer alternative
> wares to the public (1986: 28).

Within British public service broadcasting such views found little favour, but
they were meat and drink to Rupert Murdoch, whom Thatcher did everything
within her power to allow to enter the
broadcasting arena. By 1989, he was
already well enough established within
British television to be invited to give the
prestigious McTaggart Lecture at the
Edinburgh Television Festival, an opportunity he took to extol the benefits of the
market to freedom of expression:

Across the world there is a realisation that only market economies can deliver both political freedom and economic well-being, whether they be free-market economies of the right or social-market economies of the left. The freeing of broadcasting in this country is very much part of this democratic revolution and an essential step forward into the Information Age with its golden promise. It means freeing television from the lie of spectrum scarcity; freeing it from entry by any private or public enterprise which thinks it has something people might like to watch; freeing it to cater to mass and minority audiences; freeing it from the bureaucrats of television and placing it in the hands of those who should control it— the people (Murdoch 2005: 138).

MARKET FUNDAMENTALISM

In order to understand why defences of freedom of expression delivered by vast corporate interests have, since the 1980s, routinely stressed the importance of 'de-regulation', we need a little background history.

In the 1980s, the West's traditional 'heavy' industries had begun to decline, and the manufacturing sector was increasingly giving way to the service sector. Governments began to perceive the communications industries as increasingly central to the success of contemporary capitalism—both as transmitters of information of all kinds (and especially money) and as sources of jobs and hence tax revenue. Their employees were also perceived by right-wing governments, such as Thatcher's, as a good deal less 'militant' and more compliant than miners and steel-workers. At the same time, as their traditional markets became increasingly saturated, the major industrial players cast around to develop new products and services, and to enter new markets both at home and abroad. The electronic media sector looked particularly inviting, not least as new technological developments such as cable and satellite appeared to spell the end of broadcasting as a 'natural monopoly'—something that had always underpinned arguments for public service broadcasting in Europe. Meanwhile, the future possibilities for financial gain offered by 'convergence', in other words the coming together of telecommunications, broadcasting and computing, or, to put it another way, the telephone, the television and the home computer, looked like an absolute gold mine. However, to develop the necessary technology and infrastructure would take considerable capital investment, and the last thing the new media providers wanted was to be saddled with what they perceived as onerous public service requirements. Thus, in return for their capital investment, the new arrivals demanded that the broadcast and telecommunications sectors be 'de-regulated'—or rather *re-regulated* according to business-friendly principles. In a UK led by a government animated by detestation of all things public, they were of course knocking at a wide-open door.

In this vision of things, society is perceived as consisting primarily of a network of providers and recipients of goods and services. Communication services of all kinds increasingly come to be seen as commodities first and foremost, as opposed to public utilities, with private profitability taking precedence over public accessibility. Media audiences are viewed not as citizens with the right to be informed but as consumption units to whom goods and services need to be sold. This attitude was expressed in its crudest and most crass form by the head of the Federal Communications Commission, Mark Fowler, in 1984 when he stated that 'Television is just another appliance. It's a toaster with pictures' (quoted in Croteau and Hoynes 2006: 27). As Sue Curry Jansen puts it:

> Under information-capitalism, the market-place of ideas is no longer a public utility which serves all who seek its goods. Increasingly it becomes a private enterprise which serves only those who can afford to pay a price for the commodities it markets to citizen/shoppers. Under this new system of capitalism, the production of knowledge becomes a basic industry like the production of oil, steel and transportation (1991: 168).

MARKET CENSORSHIP

The problem with the argument that a free market media system is the most effective guarantor of freedom of expression is that such a system contains all the same defects as the market system in general. In particular, 'free market' philosophy is notoriously blind to the fact that access to the market is heavily skewed by already existing inequalities in society among both producers and consumers: the media marketplace is no more open to everyone who wishes to communicate their ideas than is the wider market to anyone who wants to sell goods and services. Furthermore, making information available to people is an activity of a quite different order from making available, say, cans of peas, in that it is essentially a *social good*. It thus matters greatly that the communications market by no means guarantees that everyone's tastes will be catered for; that certain kinds of material are indeed widely disseminated by 'free market' media but that others hardly figure at all; and that differences in the availability of ideas have little to do with their social worth and everything to do with their profitability—in particular their attractiveness to advertisers, who are the real drivers of such a system. Unrestricted competition by no means necessarily ensures that new producers are free to enter the marketplace, and media markets in particular are notoriously 'uncontestable' because of the high levels of investment needed for entry. Furthermore, existing players in the market, far from welcoming new competitors with open arms, as the 'free market' theory would suggest, do their absolute utmost to strangle them at birth through various forms of predation. For example, when in 1987 Robert Maxwell launched UK's first 24-hour newspaper, the *London Daily News*, Associated Newspapers, who owned London's monopoly paper the *Evening Standard*, immediately launched a 'spoiler' in the form of the *Evening News* which, needless to say, vanished the moment the *London Daily News* collapsed. Similarly, when in 2006 Rupert Murdoch's News International launched the freesheet *thelondonpaper* it found itself joined on the street remarkably quickly by Associated's all too aptly titled *London Lite*.

Equally, as the 'de-regulation' of broadcasting in countries as varied as New Zealand, Italy and the UK has conclusively demonstrated, cut-throat competition for audiences and advertisers does not encourage the blooming of a thousand flowers, but the pursuit of the lowest common denominator and the sidelining of minority tastes and views. In fact, it leads straight to what no less an advocate of the 'free market' than J. S. Mill called the tyranny of the majority. As he put it:

Protection, therefore, against the tyranny of the magistrate is not enough; there needs [to be] protection also against the tyranny of the prevailing opinion and feeling, against the tendency of society to impose, by other means than civil penalties, its own ideas and practices as rules of conduct on those who dissent from them; to fetter the development and, if possible, prevent the formation of any individuality not in harmony with its ways, and compel all characters to fashion themselves upon the model of its own. There is a limit to the legitimate interference of collective opinion with individual independence; and to find that limit, and maintain it against encroachment, is as indispensable to a good condition of human affairs as protection against political despotism (1985: 63).

The increasing privatization of information—of all kinds, and in a broad sense—means that what was once available as part of a citizen's right to know, or as part of their cultural heritage, starts to become available only at a price. Poorer consumers, in particular, may, under the combined influences of advertising, peer pressure and, in the case of parents, pester power, be tempted to spend far more than they can afford in order to keep up with the latest hardware and software. Snobs may sneer, but the fact remains that if the poor fail to buy into this market then they risk becoming victims of the digital divide or information gap, and thus more socially disadvantaged and excluded than ever. And so the world becomes ineluctably divided into the information rich and the information poor, with a direct, causal relationship between the amount of social and financial capital that people possess.

The argument that 'de-regulating' the communications market increases freedom of expression by 'giving people what they want' was never more eloquently demolished than by the Pilkington Report on British broadcasting in 1960, long before the current 'de-regulatory' vogue. As the *Report of the Committee on Broadcasting* put it:

> 'To give the public what it wants' is a misleading phrase: misleading because as commonly used it has the appearance of an appeal to democratic principle but the appearance is deceptive. It is in fact patronising and arrogant, in that it claims to know what the public is, but defines it as no more than the mass audience; and in that it claims to know what it wants but limits its choice to the average of experience. In this sense, we reject it utterly. If there is a sense in which it should be used, it is this: what the public wants and what it

has the right to get is freedom to
choose from the widest range of programme matter. Anything less than
that is deprivation (1960: 17–18).

The final line of the Pilkington Committee's judgement suggests that 'de-regulating'
the media, far from leading to a greater vari-
ety of media provision, may, in effect, result
in a narrowing of choice. This limits both
the freedom of those working in the media
to produce a wide range of diverse material,
and the freedom of audiences to access such
material. In other words, 'de-regulation' can
actually lead to a form of market censorship.

The idea that freedom of expression
can actually be limited by the market does,
however, tend to meet resistance for a
number of reasons. First, and most obviously, it is routinely trashed by the commercial media themselves. However, such
criticism is so far from being disinterested
as not to merit serious consideration.

Second, and much more substantially, it is still widely assumed that arguments that hold good for the freedom of individual expression must also be valid for large-scale commercial communication. And third, such ideas find it difficult to make headway in a culture in which the state is still seen as the main agent of censorship.

'THE PUBLIC REGULATION OF WEALTH-BASED SPEECH'

On the second point it is, as noted earlier, all too often overlooked that the much-cited US First Amendment does indeed make the distinction between freedom of speech and of the press, which today can be taken to include the rest of the media as well. And it does so for good reason. As Robert McChesney argues:

> It is one thing to assure individuals of the right to say whatever they please

without fear of government regulation or worse. This is a right that can be enjoyed by everyone on a relatively equal basis. Anyone can find a street corner to stand on to pontificate. It is another thing to say that any individual has the right to establish a free press to disseminate free speech industrially to a broader audience than could be reached by the spoken word. Here, to the extent that the effective capacity to engage in a free press is quite low for a significant portion of the population, the free speech analogy weakens. Moreover, those with the capacity to engage in a free press are in a position to determine who is empowered to disseminate speech to the great mass of the citizens and who is not. This accords special privileges to some citizens who can then dominate public debate (1999: 269).

The argument that the state is the main agent of censorship has been particularly heavily laboured in the US, where the major media interests have increasingly insisted that the First Amendment prevents only the state from regulating the communications system; in their view, moreover, this prohibition also prevents it from intervening in the system in order to try to remedy market failures of one kind or another. However—and this argument applies to any highly mediatized society—it is extremely hard to see why, in societies dominated by vast corporate interests, businesses should be any more trusted than governments when it comes to safeguarding freedom of expression, public debate and the integrity of the media. Admittedly, in the wake of 9/11, the UK and US governments have used the excuse of the 'war on terror' to clip considerably the coinage of civil liberties, freedom of expression most certainly included, but it must be stressed that this significant increase in state surveillance has been greatly facilitated by the terrorist *grande peur* whipped up on both sides of the Atlantic by vociferously right-wing media organizations, most notably Murdoch's Fox News in the US and his newspapers in the UK. Here, then, resolutely private media have actually helped to legitimate various forms of state censorship.

In this respect, it's also important to remember that, in March 1994, after certain news items about China on BBC World had upset the country's rulers, with whom Murdoch was trying to do business, he simply threw the channel off his Star satellite service so that it could no longer be received in China. Similarly, when, in 1998, he discovered that one of his publishing companies, HarperCollins, was publishing Chris Patten's account of his days as the last British Governor of Hong Kong, an account not exactly flattering to the Chinese, he

peremptorily cancelled Patten's contract.
But Murdoch is also an agent of market
censorship in that while he may have increased the *number* of channels available to
UK viewers, he has also, through forcing
public service broadcasters to compete with
him on his own commercial terms, con-
tributed greatly to narrowing the *range* of
programming available on UK television;
the Bruce Springsteen song '57 Channels
(and Nothin' On)' springs immediately to
mind. And in 2006, his attempt to interfere
in, or rather depress, the fortunes of ITV—
a rival to his BSkyB—by buying a 17.9 per
cent stake in it, caused *Guardian* columnist
Polly Toynbee on the BBC *Question Time*
programme to call him 'the most perni-
cious force in the country by far'—for
which she was tumultuously applauded—
and David Puttnam to warn that 'this can
only lead to a further and unprecedented
erosion of plurality within the British
media'.

Nor is it exactly clear why media businesses, which are now some of the most powerful corporate players in the world, should be absolved from any social responsibilities whatsoever. In fact, as Stephen Holmes puts it:

> The unrestricted freedom of the press is actually the unreviewable power of the press, the arbitrary power of an unelected minority to inflict harms free from any rule or regulation . . . For all its immunity to political censorship, the press cannot pretend to a liberty from all the obligations of mutual self-constraint imposed by the social contract (1990: 36–7).

If it insists on doing so, then there is, as Holmes notes, a very strong argument on freedom-of-expression grounds for what he calls the 'public regulation of wealth-based speech' (ibid.: 38).

In the meantime, however, as McChesney forcefully points out:

In the hands of the wealthy, the advertisers, and the corporate media, the newfangled First Amendment takes on an almost Orwellian cast. On the one hand, it defends the right of the wealthy few to effectively control our electoral system, thereby taking the risk out of democracy for the rich and making a farce out of it for most everyone else. And these semi-monopolistic corporations that brandish the Constitution as their personal property eschew any public service obligations and claim that public efforts to demand them violate their First Amendment rights, which in their view means their unimpeded ability to maximise profits regardless of their social consequences. Indeed, the media giants use their First Amendment protection not to battle for open information but to battle to protect their corporate privileges and subsidies (1999: 279).

In such a situation, media owners have ever more cynically employed arguments about the necessity of protecting a 'free press' when in fact what they are really protecting is a property right—their right to do with their media as they damn well please. But as Lichtenberg argues:

> It does not suffice simply to assert the property rights of publishers and editors against all claims to regulate the press. The publisher may say, 'It's my newspaper and I can print what I want,' but the question remains why we should accept the absolutist conception of property rights lurking in the statement as defining the publisher's role. The appeal to property rights may explain why it is the publisher—rather than the reporter or the printer or the janitor—in whom editorial authority is invested, but it does not explain why newspapers and other media organisa-

tions should be immune from regulation when other businesses are not (1990: 120).

What is particularly ironic, however, is that media corporations' attempts to hijack the First Amendment for their own commercial ends were long resisted by the US courts, which put forward a number of extremely convincing arguments both against market censorship and in favour of a conception of freedom of speech which took into account much more than the right of media owners to use their media for whatever purposes they saw fit.

A classic case is that of *Associated Press v. United States* in 1945, in which Associated Press was found guilty of breaching anti-trust laws by preventing rival newspapers from accessing its copyrighted news services. As Justice Hugo Black put it in a celebrated judgement:

[The First Amendment] rests on the assumption that the widest possible dissemination of information from diverse and antagonistic sources is essential to the welfare of the public, that a free press is a condition of a free society. Surely a command that the government itself shall not impede the free flow of ideas does not afford non-governmental combinations a refuge if they impose restraints upon that constitutionally guaranteed freedom . . . Freedom to publish means freedom for all, and not for some. Freedom to publish is guaranteed by the Constitution, but freedom to combine to keep others from publishing is not. Freedom of the press from governmental interference under the First Amendment does not sanction repression of that freedom by private interests (quoted in Barron 2004: 375).

What, crucially, the first part of Black's judgement stresses is that those concerned with freedom of expression in the modern media need to concentrate as much on the rights of audiences as on the rights of producers. In particular, we need to consider their *communicative rights*, as active citizens in a democracy, to access a wide and diverse range of information and views that will enable them to inform themselves on the main issues of the day. It cannot be stressed too strongly that, in modern societies, information is and should be treated as a public good, or as what used to be called 'the commons'. Central to such arguments for freedom of expression is not simply the media's right to 'speak' but audiences' right to listen to and *participate in* discussion and debate animated by a multiplicity of voices. After all, one of the main reasons for defending freedom of expression in the first place is that it is necessary, if people are to be informed, to be able to think and decide for themselves and generally to function as citizens of a democratic society. If the media signally fail to provide these benefits of freedom of expression, then not only is their right to exercise that freedom seriously weakened, but the notion of freedom of expression itself is inevitably cheapened and degraded.

POWER WITH RESPONSIBILITY

Power, and in particular the power to communicate with millions of people, brings with it responsibilities. As UK Conservative Prime Minister Stanley Baldwin put it in 1931 when he was being attacked by Conservative newspapers for not being Conservative enough: 'What proprietorship of these papers is aiming at is power, and power without responsibility—the prerogative of the harlot throughout the ages.'

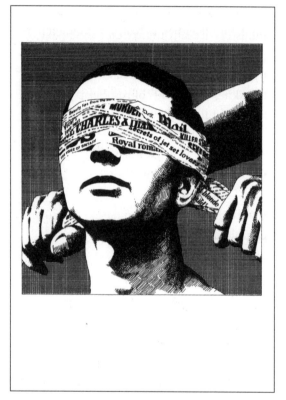

Blinded by Trivia. By permission of the Campaign for
Press and Broadcasting Freedom.

Baldwin was one of the very few prime ministers actually to take on the newspapers—and he won, decisively. Perhaps, then, we should honour Baldwin's example by asking what kinds of responsibility are attendant upon the freedom to communicate—both at an individual level and in mediated form. Most people would agree that freedom of expression is vital in a democracy—but does that necessarily mean that that freedom must be exercised, and in a completely unqualified fashion, on each and every occasion that the opportunity presents itself?

The best answer to this question is to be found in the 'big idea' of the second half of the twentieth century, namely human rights. As Rabinder Singh points out:

> Since World War Two, in particular, the age-old problem of whether there are human rights and where they come

> from—whether from pure reason, natu-
> ral law, divine origin or universal cus-
> tom—has been largely avoided, if not
> resolved, by the social fact that the in-
> ternational community has come to ac-
> cept a set of principles as being of
> global application (1997: 38).

Or as Conor Gearty puts it:

> The criticisms of the philosophers (old
> and modern) have been met, implicitly
> if not explicitly, and a large gap has
> opened up between the *idea* of human
> rights and the *fact* of human rights *law*.
> The Universal Declaration of Human
> Rights is just that—a declaration, rather
> than a piece of legislation in the tradi-
> tional sense, or even in the international
> law sense. Its pronouncement changed
> nothing in any kind of tangible way. It is
> a reaffirmation of human dignity in-
> tended to inform rather than predeter-
> mine political debate (2006: 19).

In Europe, the human rights framework was put into place in 1953 by the European Convention on Human Rights. The UK was the first signatory, but its provisions were not adopted by parliament until 1998 when the Human Rights Act was passed.

As one of the Convention's strongest supporters, Lord Lester QC, stresses, the Convention is 'an instrument designed to maintain and promote the ideals and values of a democratic society' (Lester and Pannick 1999: 67). Entirely unsurprisingly, then, it encompasses the ideal and value of freedom of expression. Thus Article 10 states that:

> Everyone has the right to freedom of expression. This right shall include freedom to hold opinions and to receive and impart information and ideas without interference by public authority and regardless of frontiers.

At the same time, however, it is crucial to note that the second paragraph of Article 10 adds:

> The exercise of these freedoms, since it carries with it duties and responsibilities, may be subject to such formalities, conditions, restrictions or penalties as are prescribed by law and are necessary in a democratic society, in the interests of national security, territorial integrity or public safety, for the prevention of disorder or crime, for the protection of health or morals, for the protection of the reputation or the rights of others, for preventing the disclosure of information received in confidence, or for maintaining the authority and impartiality of the judiciary.

Also highly significant in the context of freedom of expression is Article 8, which states that:

> Everyone has the right to respect for
> his private and family life, his home
> and his correspondence.

This clearly has a bearing on, *inter alia*, what the media may and may not report.

From the above, it is immediately obvious that rights such as these are conditional as opposed to absolute—such as the right not to be subjected to torture or to inhuman or degrading treatment or punishment. In cases involving such rights, both domestic courts and, if it ultimately becomes involved in such cases, the European Court of Human Rights, have to carry out a very delicate balancing exercise to determine whether a Convention right has been *justifiably* interfered with. In particular, the courts must be satisfied that any restriction of a person's conditional rights was necessary—and not simply desirable, useful or convenient—in a democratic society; for this to be so, it must meet a pressing social need. In this respect, Lester helpfully quotes a European Court judgement to the effect that when courts deliberate on matters concerning the Convention, they should strive to give effect to its central   animating principle and seek to strike a 'fair balance . . . between the demands of the general interest of the community and the requirements of the protection of the individual's fundamental rights' (ibid.: 68).

IN CONCLUSION

We began with a number of ringing endorsements of freedom of expression, so let us close with an equally ringing, but significantly more qualified one. This was handed down in 1986 when the European Court of Human Rights overturned a verdict of criminal libel passed by an Austrian court on the editor of a magazine which had published allegations about the then Chancellor, Bruno Kreisky. The Court argued that:

> [Freedom of expression] constitutes
> one of the essential foundations of a
> democratic society and one of the basic
> conditions for its progress and for each
> individual's self-fulfilment. Subject to
> paragraph 2, it is applicable not only to
> 'information' or 'ideas' that are favourably received or regarded as inoffensive or as a matter of indifference, but
> also those that offend, shock or disturb.
> Such are the demands of that pluralism, tolerance and broadmindedness
> without which there is no 'democratic
> society'. These principles are of particular importance as far as the press is
> concerned. Whilst the press must not
> overstep the bounds set, *inter alia*, for
> the 'protection of the reputation of
> others', it is nonetheless incumbent on

it to impart information and ideas on political issues just as on those in other areas of public interest. Not only does the press have the task of imparting such information and ideas: the public also has a right to receive them . . . Freedom of the press furthermore affords the public one of the best means of discovering and forming an opinion of the ideas and attitudes of political leaders. More generally, freedom of political debate is at the very core of the concept of a democratic society which prevails throughout the convention (quoted in Gearty 2006: 44).

With its stress on the centrality of the media to the democratic process, the importance of protecting unpopular ideas as well as received opinion, the responsibilities as well as the rights of the media, the justifiable limits on freedom of expression and the right of the public to be properly informed, nothing could sum up more clearly and succinctly than this judgement all the arguments put forward in this essay for a concept of freedom of expression appropriate to democratic societies in the media age.

BIBLIOGRAPHY

BARENDT, Eric (2005), *Media Law*, Oxford: Oxford University Press.

BARRON, James A. (2004), 'Access to the Press: a New First Amendment Right', in Robert W. McChesney, and Ben Scott (eds), *Our Unfree Press*: *100 Years of Radical Media Criticism*, New York: The New Press.

CROTEAU, David and Hoynes, William (2006), *The Business of Media*: *Corporate Media and the Public Interest*, Thousand Oaks, CA: Pine Forge Press.

CURRAN, James and Seaton, Jean (2003, sixth edition), *Power Without Responsibility*: *the Press, Broadcasting and New Media in Britain*, London: Routledge.

DE JONGH, Nicholas (2000), *Politics, Prudery and Perversions*: *the Censoring of the English Stage 1901-1968*, London: Methuen.

EVANS, B Ifor (1944), 'Milton and the Modern Press', in Hermon Ould (ed.), *Freedom of Expression*: *a Symposium*, London: Hutchinson International Authors Ltd, pp. 26–9.

GEARTY, Conor (2006), *Principles of Human Rights Adjudication*, Oxford: Oxford University Press.

HARGREAVES, Robert (2002), *The First Freedom: a History of Free Speech*, Stroud: Sutton Publishing.

HILL, Christopher (1977), *Milton and the English Revolution*, London: Faber and Faber.

HOLMES, Stephen (1990), 'Liberal Constraints on Private Power? Reflections on the Origins and Rationale of Access Regulation', in Judith Lichtenberg (ed.), *Democracy and the Mass Media*, Cambridge: Cambridge University Press.

HUME, David (1994), *Political Writings*, Stuart D. Warner and Donald W. Livingston (eds), Indianapolis: Hacket Publishing Company

JANSEN, Sue Curry (1991), *Censorship: the Knot that Binds Power and Knowledge*, Oxford: Oxford University Press.

JEFFERSON, Thomas (1993), *The Life and Selected Writings of Thomas Jefferson*, Adrienne Koch and William Peden (eds), New York: Random House.

KEANE, John (1991), *The Media and Democracy*, Cambridge: Polity.

—— (1996), *Tom Paine: a Political Life*, London: Bloomsbury.

LESTER, Anthony and Pannick, David (1999), *Human Rights Law and Practice*, London: Butterworths.

LICHTENBERG, Judith (1990), 'Foundations and Limits of Freedom of the Press', in Judith Lichtenberg (ed.), *Democracy and the Mass Media*, Cambridge: Cambridge University Press.

MAYER, David N. (1994), *The Constitutional Thought of Thomas Jefferson*, Charlottesville: University Press of Virginia.

McCHESNEY, Robert (1999), *Rich Media, Poor Democracy*: *Communication Politics in Dubious Times*, New York: The New Press.

MILL, John Stuart (1965), *Collected Works: John Stuart Mill*: *Volume III*, Toronto: University of Toronto Press.

—— (1985), *On Liberty*, London: Penguin.

MILTON, John (1990), *Complete English Poems, Of Education, Areopagitica*, Gordon Campbell (ed.), London: J. M. Dent and Sons Ltd.

MURDOCH, Rupert (2005), 'Freedom in Broadcasting', in Bob Franklin (ed.), *Television Policy*: *the MacTaggart Lectures*, Edinburgh: Edinburgh University Press.

PAINE, Tom (1806), 'Liberty of the press', www.uark.edu/depts/comminfo/cambridge/tpliberty.html

Report of the Committee on Broadcasting (1960), London: HMSO.

Report of the Committee on Financing the BBC (1986), London: HMSO

RILEY, Jonathan (1998), *Mill on Liberty*, London: Routledge.

ROBERTSON, Geoffrey and Nicol, Andrew (2002), *Robertson and Nicol on Media Law*, London: Sweet and Maxwell.

SINGH, Rabinder (1997), *The Future of Human Rights in the United Kingdom: Essays on Law and Practice*, Oxford: Hart Publishing.

WILLIAMSON, Audrey (1973), *Thomas Paine: His Life, Work and Times*, London: George Allen and Unwin Ltd.